1   BODY SYSTEMS

To exercise we need all these body systems working. How does each body system help us with our exercise?

Muscle-Skeleton
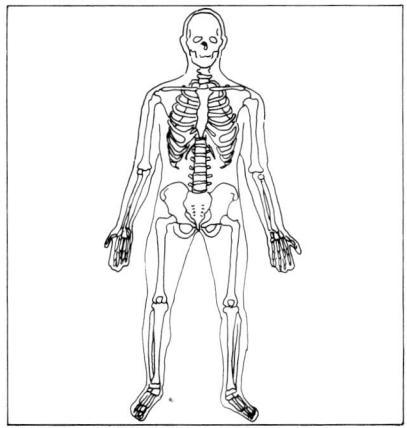

Cardiovascular
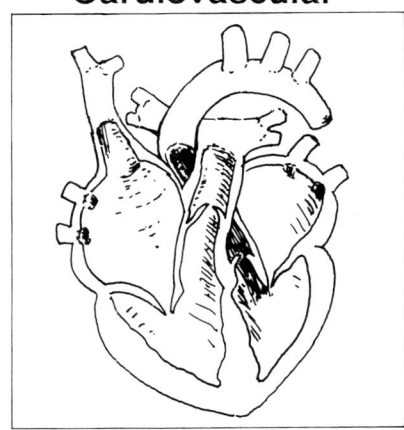

Nervous
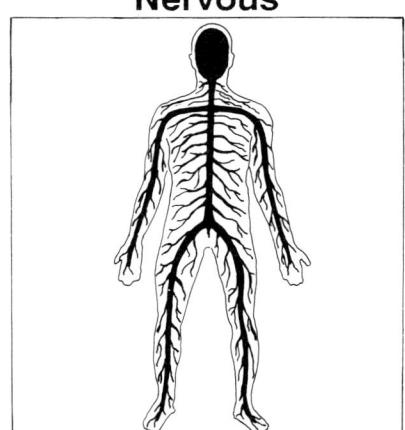

Respiratory
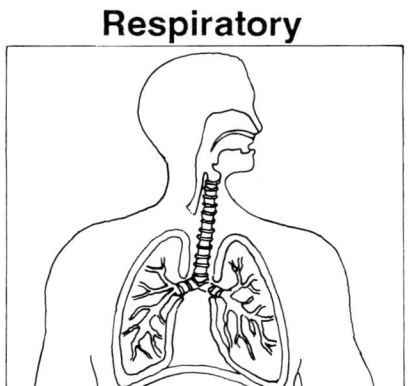

Digestive
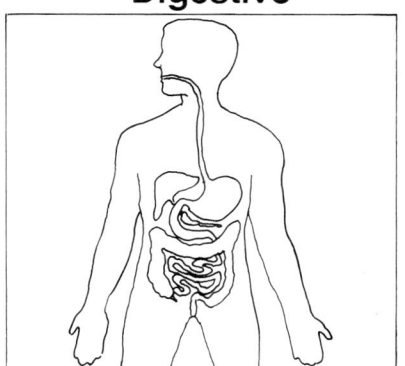

Muscle-Skeleton..

....

Nervous...

....

Cardiovascular...

....

Respiratory..

....

Digestive...

....

Teacher's Notes

Body Systems

Muscular-Skeletal Systems

The human skeleton consists of the skull, the backbone, the ribs, the shoulder girdle, the bones of the upper limbs, the pelvis and the bones of the lower limbs. The skeleton provides the framework which maintains our body shape. The bones are the structures through which movement is made.

Muscles that cover the skeleton are known as skeletal muscles. The body's power to hold itself upright and to move is due to the skeletal muscles.

Nervous System

The nervous system consists of the brain, the spinal cord and the peripheral, free-running nerves which supply all parts of the body. The nervous system controls the movements through our muscles.

Cardiovascular System

The heart distributes blood to the various parts of the body through a system of tubes. Arteries convey blood away from the heart while veins bring blood to the heart. The cardiovascular system carries oxygen and dissolved nutrients to all body parts and transports waste products away from working muscles.

Respiratory System

The respiratory system consists of the air passages and the lungs. This system provides oxygen for the blood and also removes waste products such as carbon dioxide from the body.

Digestive System

The digestive system controls the passage of food through the body. This system processes food and fluids so they can be utilised by the various organs of the body along with working muscles. Food absorbed by the blood provides energy for the muscles.

Carefully cut out the bones and make a SKELETON.

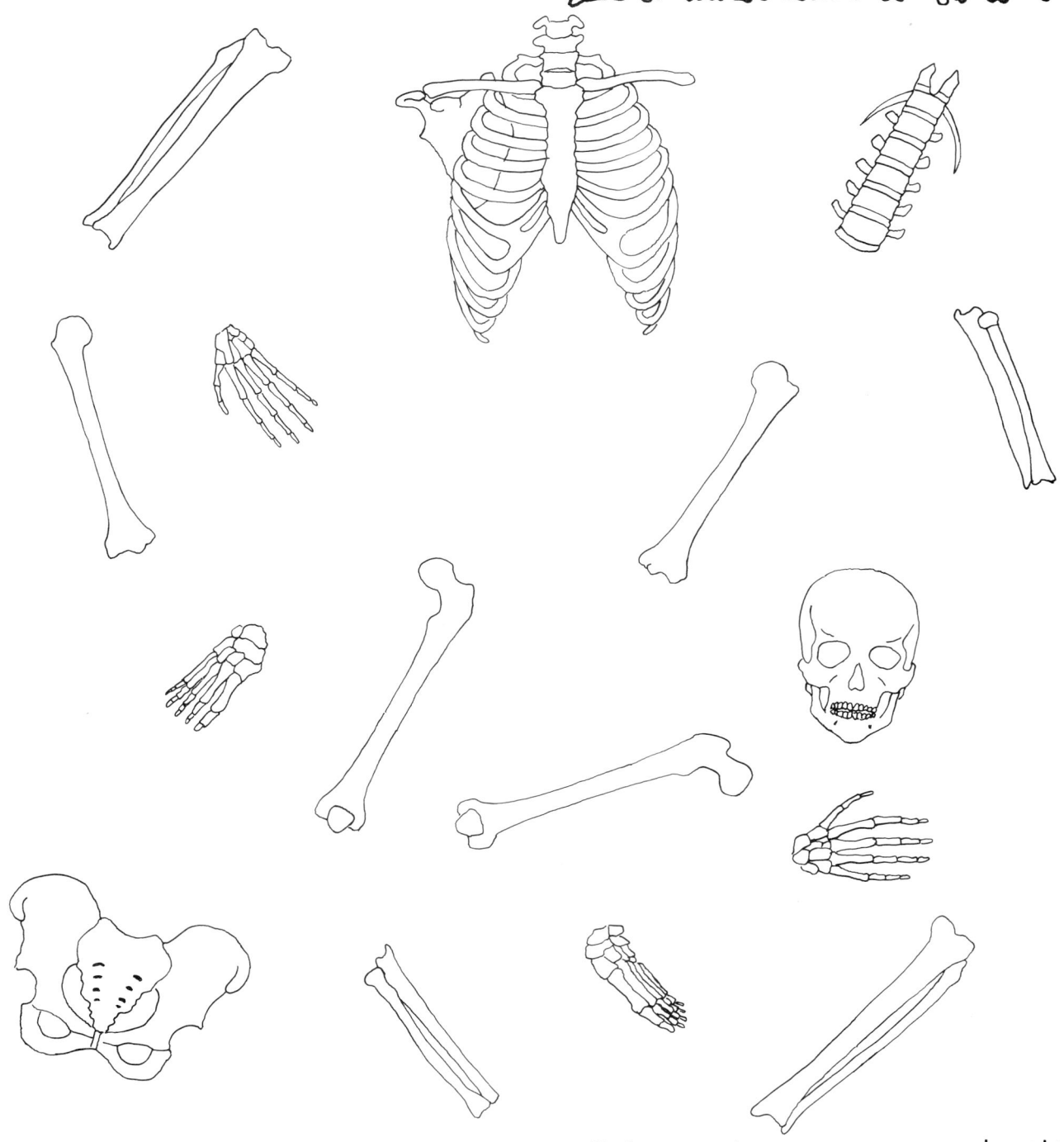

When you have made your skeleton, paste it down onto some paper and match these names with the bones.

| spine | tibia | ribs | skull |
| pelvis | femur | humerus | |

3 | HOW BONES HELP US   Name.......................

The bones which make up the skeleton are a very important part of the body.
Bones give our body shape.
In the box below draw a picture of your body without bones.

 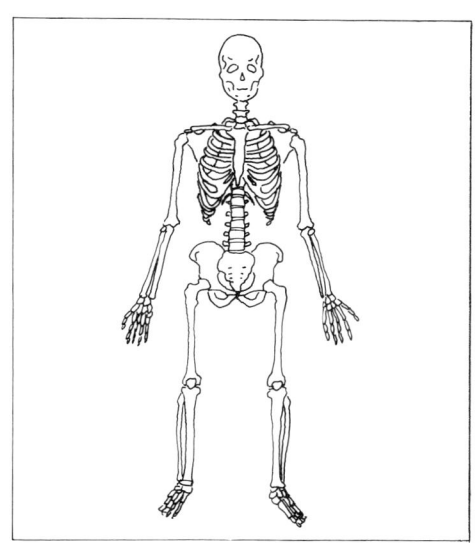

Bones help to protect parts of the body like the heart and the brain.
Which bones protect:

(a) the heart? ....
(b) the lungs? ....
(c) the brain? ....
(d) the spinal cord? ....

Bones help us to move.

Where is the longest bone in our body?

....

Where is the smallest bone in our body?

....

Teacher's Notes

How Bones Help Us

The longest bone is the femur: it is located in the upper part of the leg.

The smallest bone is the stapes which is located in the middle ear. It is about 6-7 mm in length.

Did you know that:

- nearly half of your body weight is made up of muscles?
- every movement you make involves muscles?
- muscles come in different sizes?
- every muscle has a partner?

Try these activities.

Make a tight fist with one of your
hands. Use the other hand to feel
the different muscles in your arm.

Sit with your legs stretched out in front of you. Point your toes away from you.
Now you can see and feel some of the muscles in your legs.

What differences do you notice between your arm and leg muscles? ....
....
Which muscles do you think are stronger, your leg or arm muscles? Why? ....
....

Teacher's Notes

Muscles, Muscles

In this activity children should come to the realization that muscles vary in size and shape. The size of muscles relates to the amount of strength muscles exhibit. Weight training aimed at increasing muscle strength leads to an increase in the size of muscles.

Name........................

Muscles cover our bones. They help us to move, give us shape and protect the bones and organs in our body.

Which picture looks most like your body shape,

this

Draw and colour in some muscles on this skeleton.

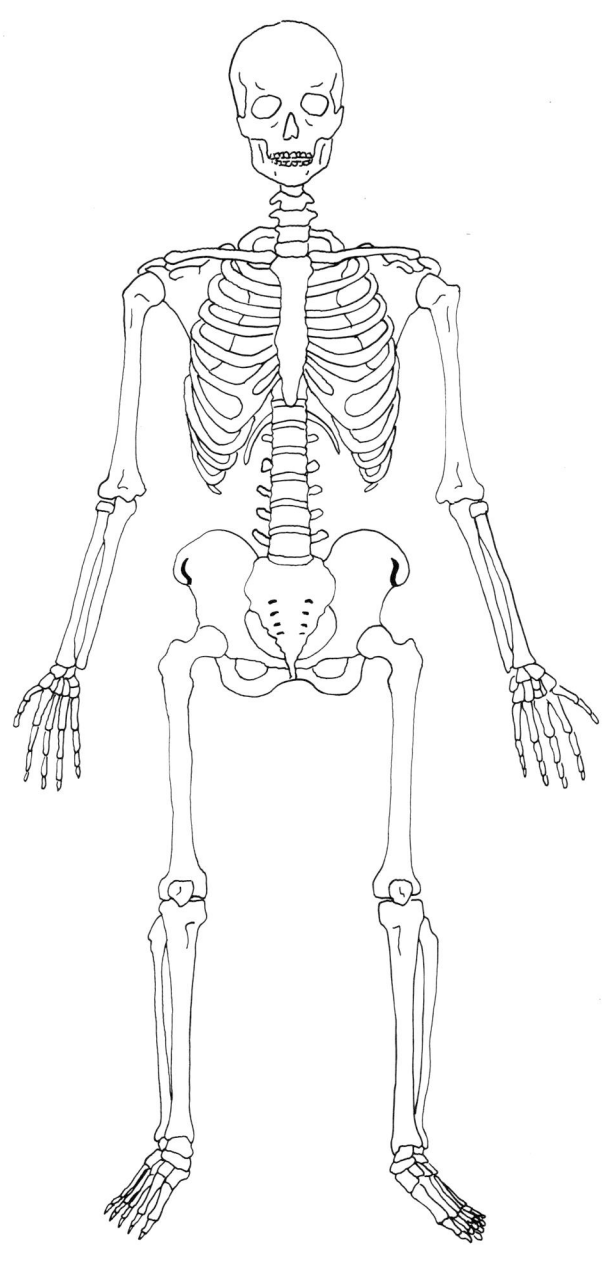

or this?

WHAT MUSCLE IS THAT?   Name........................

Every muscle has a name. Most of the muscles have names which are difficult to remember. To make it easier to remember them, we sometimes use names which are more simple.

Can you match the easy names in the list with the muscles shown in the pictures below?

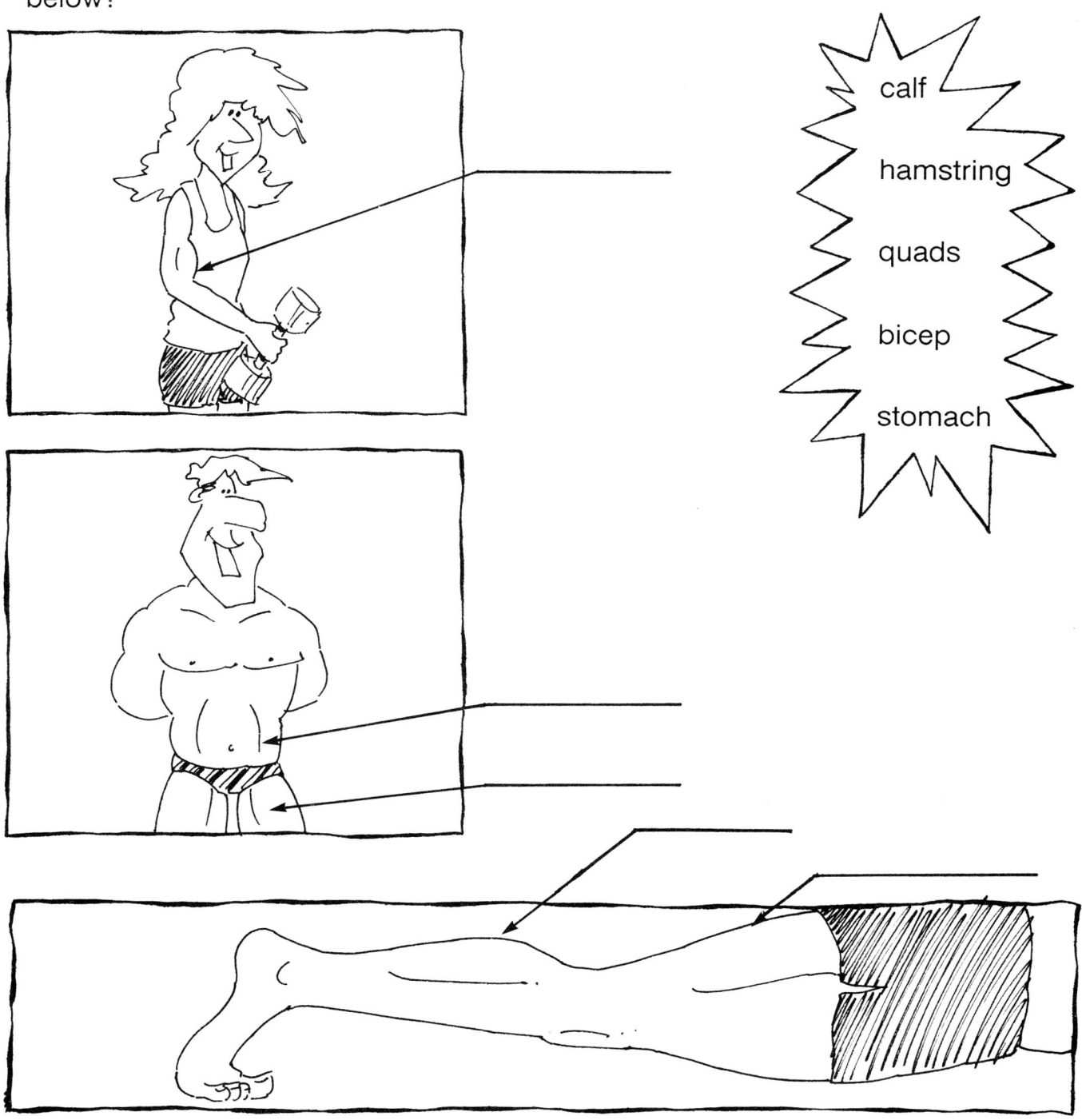

calf

hamstring

quads

bicep

stomach

Your muscles always work in pairs.

Here is an experiment for you to try.
You will need:

- 2 small blocks of wood
- 2 pieces of elastic
- 4 thumb tacks

What to do.

Tack the pieces of elastic to the blocks of wood like this:

Now change the blocks of wood to the position shown below.

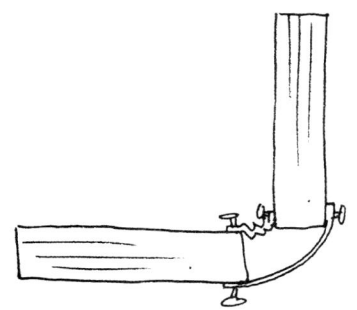

Write a description of what happened to the piece of elastic. ....
....
....
....

The muscles in your body work the same way. As some muscles stretch, others shorten to allow you to move.

Here is something else for you to try.

Place one hand around the front of your upper arm. Feel what happens when you bend and straighten your elbow. Try it again, this time with your hand at the back of your arm near your arm pit.

Describe what you felt.
....
....
....
....

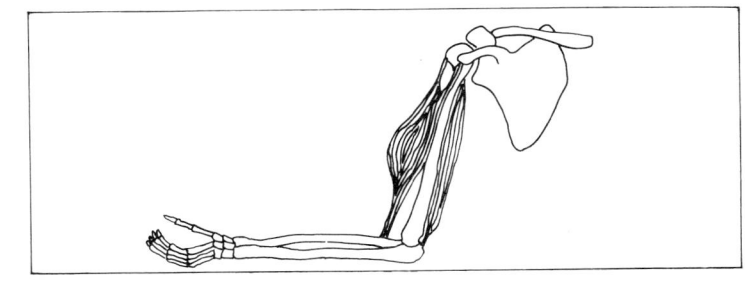

Teacher's Notes

How Do Muscles Work?

Muscles work in pairs. With movement one muscle contracts, it changes shape becoming shorter and thicker, while its partner extends or stretches beyond its normal length.

All movements in the body involve muscular contractions. When muscles lose elasticity, movement is restricted, as the particular muscles will not extend or stretch sufficiently. Exercises in flexibility assist muscles to regain elasticity which permits a greater range of movement at the joints.

Did you know that there are three different types of muscles?

One type is found in our arms and legs and in other parts of our body as well. It is called **skeleton muscle**. You have control over these muscles and can make them work when you want them to.

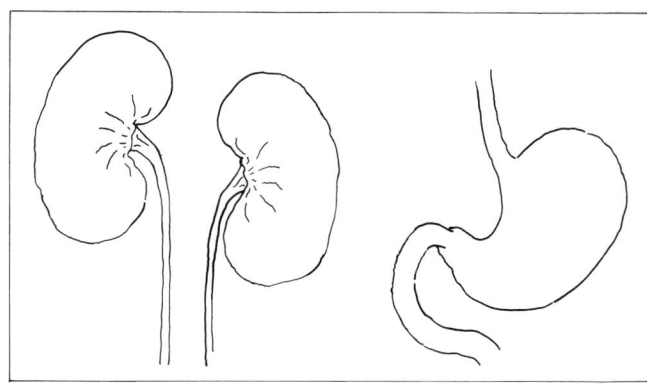

Another type of muscle is found in our stomach and body organs. These muscles are active all the time. We cannot make them start or stop.

The third type of muscle is only found in the heart. It is called **heart muscle**. Did you know the heart is a muscle?

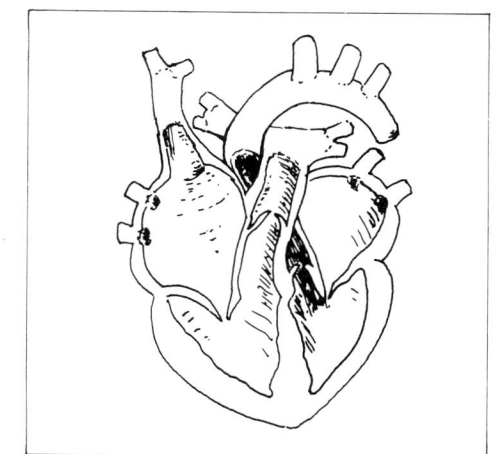

In the boxes below, draw a picture which shows:

(a) when your skeleton muscles are at work
(b) when your skeleton muscles are at rest.

Complete the following activities with a partner.

Using a stopwatch (or the second hand on a wristwatch) count how many times each of you breathes in a minute.

You ....

Your partner ....

Now do some exercise.

Count each other's breaths again for one minute.

You ....

Your partner ....

What did you notice? ....

....

Why do you think this happens? ....

....

Teacher's Notes

The Air We Breathe

When the body exercises, oxygen is required by the working muscles. Conversely, working muscles produce greater amounts of carbon dioxide which needs to be removed from the muscles, carried back to the lungs and expired. The breathing rate quickens to supply the blood with greater amounts of oxygen which is absorbed and carried to the muscles. A faster breathing rate is also required to expire greater amounts of carbon dioxide that was breathed in, as well as that produced by the active muscles.

Your pulse lets you know how fast your heart beats.

Count your pulse while you rest.

Now do some exercise.

Count your pulse over a minute again.

What do you notice? ....

....

....

....

Teacher's Notes

Check Your Pulse

There are two main areas on the body where a pulse can be felt. One is found on the wrist. It is called the **radial pulse**. The other place is on the side of the neck where the carotid artery runs. This pulse is called the **carotid pulse**. For children, the carotid pulse is the better one to use as it is a strong pulse and can be easily located.

When children feel their pulse they are feeling the blood being pushed in surges through the particular artery. The surges of blood correspond directly to the heart contractions.

A pulse is usually taken for only fifteen seconds, especially after exercise. If taken over a full minute the heart rate slows when exercise ceases. The difference in the heart rate at the beginning of the minute and at the end would be quite significant, leading to an inaccurate indication of the heart rate when the person was exercising.

TEST YOURSELF   **Name......................**

Fill in the blank spaces by choosing the correct word from the box below.

Pumps blood around your body. ....

The bones in your body, together are called a ....

The name of a muscle which is found in your arm. ....

These bones protect your heart and lungs. ....

Lungs do the .... for your body.

Where is the longest bone in your body? ....

The skull helps to protect our ....

Bones and .... help us to move.

Your .... lets you know how fast your heart is beating.

.... helps to keep your body fit.

pulse	exercise	brain	skeleton	leg
breathing	ribs	muscles	heart	bicep

Name.......................

Easy activities are those which require little effort. These include walking, sitting and school work.

Medium activities are those which cause slight sweating and faster breathing, such as walking fast, dancing and riding a bike slowly.

Hard activities are those where the heart beats quickly, breathing is fast and there is a lot of sweating. Riding a bike quickly and playing games which involve a lot of running such as netball, football and tennis are difficult activities.

Complete the box below by writing down five activities that you did yesterday. Decide whether they were easy, medium or hard activities.

Activity	Level of difficulty

Do you think you lead an active lifestyle? Why? ....

....

....

....

COULD YOU BE MORE ACTIVE?   Name.......................

Tick (✓) the activities which involve exercise and would help you to keep fit.

Are you active enough to get fit and to stay that way? Why? ....

....

....

....

....

....

Some people are very active, other people are not.
Which type of person are you? ....

Fill out the table below for one week. Write down every physical activity that you do. Don't count walking around at home or at school.

Monday	
Tuesday	
Wednesday	
Thursday	
Friday	
Saturday	
Sunday	

Look at how active you were during the week. Which picture is most like you:

this   **or this?**

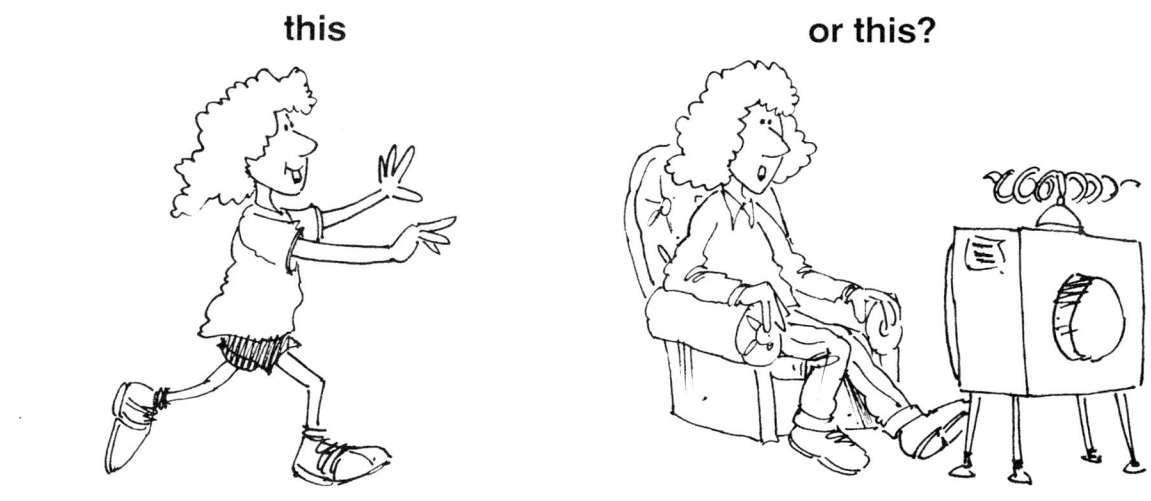

On which day were you most active? ....
On which day were you least active? ....
Were you surprised at how much or how little you did? Why? ....

....

....

....

Are you an active person? Why?...

....

....

....

Here are some tests for you to try.

(a) Sit with your legs stretched out in front of you and touch your toes.

(b) Do fifteen sit-ups with your knees bent.

(c) Jump rope for one minute without stopping.

(d) Jog around your school oval once without stopping.

(e) Lean against a bench and do ten push-ups.

How many of the five tests could you do? ....

Is there anything you could do to improve your fitness level? ....

....

....

....

....

....

Fill in the missing words.

Car...io.........c.........r   end...r...nce
is the ability of the heart to keep the
muscles supplied with oxygen and to
keep the body working.

Fl...x...b.........ty means free movement
of the joints.

St.........gth means the force your muscles
can produce.

Mus......l...r   end.........nce is the
ability of the muscles to keep
working for a long time.

Teacher's Notes

Fitness Is...

Missing words:
Cardiovascular endurance is the ability of the heart to keep the muscles supplied with oxygen and to keep the body working.

Flexibility means free movement of the joints.

Strength means the force your muscles can produce.

Muscular endurance is the ability of the muscles to keep working for a long time.

GET YOUR BODY FIT   Name......................

Write about two different activities which could help to improve the following:

Aerobic fitness

....
....
....
....

Muscular endurance

....
....
....
....

Strength

....
....
....
....

Joint mobility

Teacher's Notes

Get Your Body Fit

Cardiovascular endurance (Aerobic fitness) is improved through activities which make the heart beat at least 150 times per minute. Aerobic fitness improves the heart which gets used to beating at a high rate for longer periods of time.

Muscular endurance is improved through activities which cause the muscles to work for increasingly long periods of time.

Muscular strength is improved when muscles are required to work strenuously in short bursts of effort. This type of activity needs to be carried out repeatedly.

Joint mobility (flexibility) is improved through stretching activities which gradually stretch muscles and ligaments. This improves their elasticity.

For children, muscle endurance can be improved by doing cardiovascular endurance activities. The activities do not need to be strenuous but should be of increasing duration.

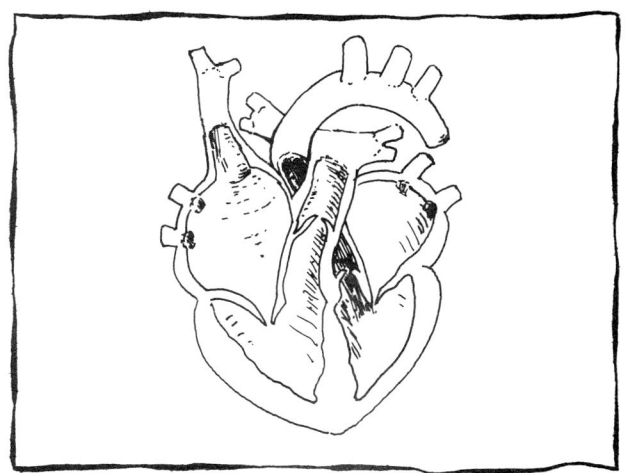

Your heart works like a pump by pushing blood, which carries oxygen, to the hard working skeleton muscles and various organs of the body.

The heart never rests.

What would happen if your heart did stop? ....

....

....

Here is something for you to try.

While you are having a rest, put one hand on the left side of your chest. You should be able to feel your heart beating, pushing blood around your body.

Now go for a jog for about one minute. When you finish place your hand on the left side of your chest. Can you feel your heart beating?

What did you notice? ....

....

Why does this happen? ....

....

Teacher's Notes

Your Heart

When exercising, the heart rate increases. This is largely due to energy production requirements. As the demand for oxygen and nutrients in the muscles increases, the heart responds by beating faster to supply the oxygen and nutrients. At the same time the blood removes increasing amounts of waste product from the muscles.

A HARD WORKING HEART   Name........................

When you are resting, your heart beats about eighty times per minute.

If you ran as fast as you could around your school, your heart rate may increase to as many as 200 beats per minute.

Here is a way to find out just how hard your heart works. Complete the table below by taking your pulse at five different times of the day over a three day period. (You may need an adult to help you take your pulse).

Time of day	Day 1	Day 2	Day 3
Waking up			
When you get to school			
The end of your lunch break			
When you get home from school			
Before bed			

When did your heart work hardest? ....
Why? ....
....

Your heart has a very important job to do. It pumps blood, food and oxygen to all parts of your body. We must make sure that the heart keeps doing its job.

How can we do this?

Remember that your heart is a muscle. When you make muscles work hard they become stronger. This will also happen to your heart when you exercise. A strong heart can do its job more easily.

Which of the following activities would most improve the strength of your heart? Why? ....

....

Draw a picture of yourself doing an activity which will make your heart stronger.

Aerobic fitness will help to keep your heart, arteries and veins strong and healthy. If you have a strong heart you won't get tired as easily when you run.

If your heart is to become stronger and healthier, aerobic activities should last longer than five minutes.

You should not do aerobic activities too quickly. It is better to be able to do them for a long time. Your heart should beat about 150 times per minute when you do aerobic activities.

Here is one type of aerobic fitness activity. Draw yourself doing some other forms of aerobic fitness activity.

Stretching our muscles can help
to keep our joints moving freely
and easily.

Can you think of three everyday
tasks where your muscles are
required to stretch?

(a) ....

(b) ....

(c) ....

Here are three rules for stretching.

| Warm-up first | Do each exercise slowly | Hold the stretch for three seconds |

Stretching is good for our muscles. How do you think it helps us in sports like
soccer, gymnastics and netball? ....

....

....

....

....

Teacher's Notes

Stretching

Improved flexibility for sport has three main benefits. The first is improved performance. An increase in the range of joint movement will allow skills to be performed at a higher level. Greater flexibility can assist in avoiding injuries. Improved elasticity permits the muscles to stretch rather than tear. Stretching also assists in reducing muscle soreness after strenuous activity.

STRETCH THOSE MUSCLES! Name.......................

Try the stretching exercises in the pictures below. Then, with a red pencil, colour in the parts of the body where the muscles are being stretched.

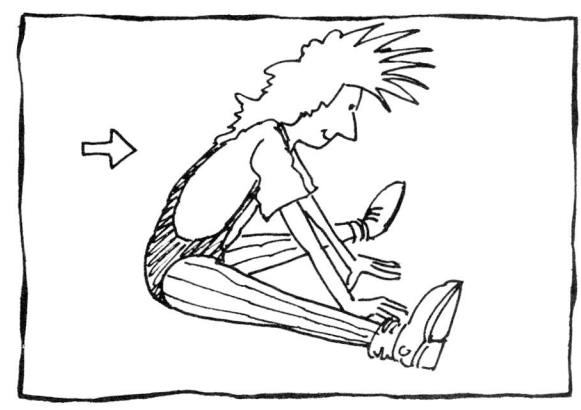

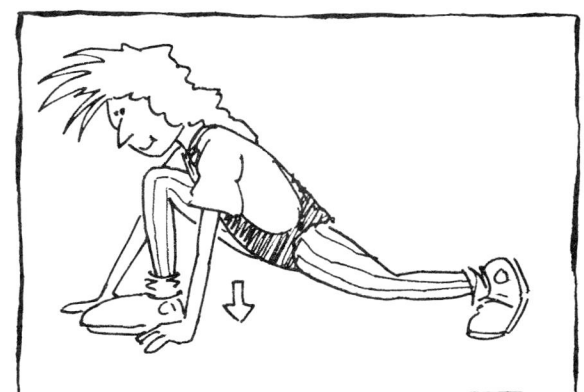

Remember!

It is important to stretch all the main muscle groups.

Stretch each muscle group slowly three times.

The force which a muscle can produce is called strength. Because of this force we are able to do certain activities.

List five things that you do each day which require muscular strength.

....

....

The stronger your muscles are, the easier it is to do certain activities. Which of the activities listed below do you think require a lot of strength to perform. Write 'yes' or 'no' in the space provided.

Running up a hill ....   Riding a bike ....
Playing marbles ....   Reading a book ....
Digging a deep hole ....   Pushing a car ....

Did you know that many people involved in certain sports do special training to make their muscles stronger?

Which muscle groups do you think each of these athletes tries to strengthen?

Sprinter ....

Rower ....

Surfer ....

Swimmer ....

Weight Lifter ....

MAKE THOSE MUSCLES STRONGER!

Name.......................

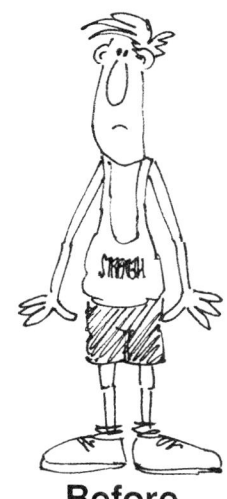

Before

After

To become stronger we need to make our muscles work very hard. To maintain our strength it is best to exercise a few times each week.

Can you think of three everyday activities that you do which make your muscles work hard? ....
....
....

Find a partner and try these strengthening activities. For your own safety it would be best if you did them on a soft surface.

Muscle endurance means being able to work your muscles for a long time without getting tired.

Test yourself!

Find a bench or a low seat. Step up onto it, one foot at a time, bringing one foot down to the ground as your other one is placed on the seat.

What did you notice about your leg muscles? ....
....
....
....
....

Here are some activities to help build up muscle endurance. Which muscle groups do you think these activities help to strengthen?

Running ....   Sit-ups ....

Swimming ....   Push-ups ....

Bike riding ....   Skating ....

Skipping ....   Climbing ....

FITNESS ACTIVITIES HELP   Name.........................

To improve the following skills, name an activity which would use:

(a) balance ....

(b) power ....

(c) coordination

....

(d) speed ....

(e) reaction time

....

Teacher's Notes

Fitness Activities Help

Motor performance skills such as balance, power, coordination, speed and reaction time can be enhanced through fitness activities.

Balance
There are two types of balance — **static** and **dynamic**. Static balance is the physical ability which enables a person to hold a stationary position. Dynamic balance is the ability to maintain balance during vigorous movement, as in hopping along on one foot or walking on stepping stones. Balance is used in everyday activities as well as in most games and sports.

Power
This can be viewed as the ability to release maximum force (strength) in the fastest possible time. Power is evident in activities such as a vertical jump, long jump and the shot put.

Speed
This can be defined as the rate at which a person can propel their body, or parts of their body through space. Speed is most obvious in sprinting activities, however it is inherent in most games and sports.

Reaction Time
This is the interval of time between the presentation of the stimulus and the initiation of the response. Starting a sprint race or catching a ball close-in in softball or cricket would require fast body responses.

Coordination
This can be defined as the effectiveness and rhythmical efficiency with which a person moves their body. The body's senses play a vital role in coordinating movements. Good examples of coordination are found in gymnastics, dance and running.

QUICK CHANGES   Name.......................

It takes practice to be able to
quickly change the speed and
direction of your movements.
This is called **agility**. Agility
is important in many team
sports.

Can you think of three sports where quick changes of speed and direction are
often necessary?

....

....

Test yourself!

To complete the following activities you will need a stopwatch and some witches'
hats or markers.

Lay your markers out as shown in the diagrams below. Make sure you leave the
right amount of space between each one.

Following the lines shown below, see how fast you can run through each course.

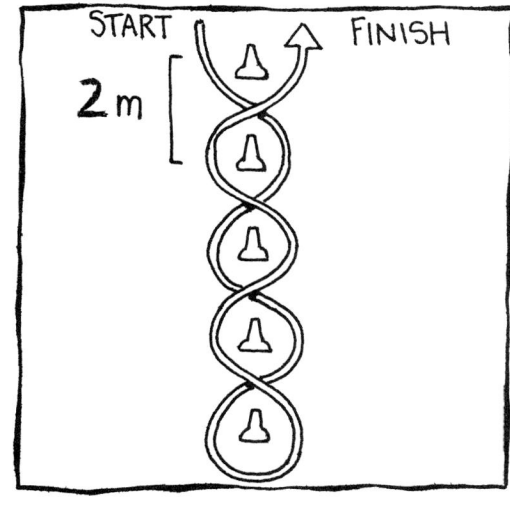

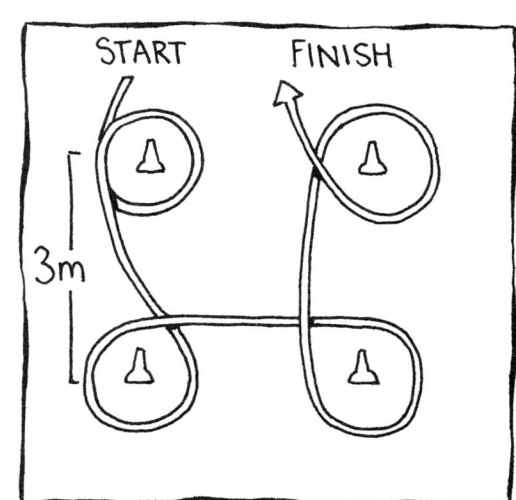

Your time: .... secs   Your time: .... secs

Name.....................

Balancing your body means that you can hold
a position without falling over.

Try this!

Can you stand on one leg? ....

For how long can you do it? ....

Try it again, this time with your eyes
shut.

Which way was it harder for you to
keep your balance? Why? ....

....

....

....

Can you think of three activities where balance is important? ....

....

....

Can you balance using only the following body parts? (For your safety, practise
on a soft surface)

(a) one knee

(b) two hands

(c) one hand and one foot

(d) one elbow and one knee

Remember!

Practice makes perfect.

Name..........................

Power does not mean exactly the same thing as strength. Power requires both strength and fast movements.

Try these activities!

Stand beside a wall.
How high can you jump
without a run-up?

.... cm

Stand with your two feet together
on a line. How far can you jump
from the line?

.... cm

What do you think you could do to make yourself more powerful? ....
....
....
....
....

HOW FAST ARE YOU?   **Name.......................**

Getting your body to move quickly from rest to activity is called **reaction**.

Try this!

To complete the following activity you will need a partner and a stopwatch. See how long it takes for you to go from lying on your back, to standing up and then running five metres.

Write down three activities where you need to react quickly.

(a) ....

(b) ....

(c) ....

Remember!

The more you practise the faster you will get.

KEEPING FIT—KEEPS YOU ALERT Name.........................

If the people in the picture above did not have senses, a serious accident may have occurred.

How many senses do we have? ....

....

....

Which senses are involved in the picture above? How? ....

....

....

....

Name some activities which would help to keep you alert. ....

....

....

....

Warm-ups get our bodies ready for fitness activities.

Warm-ups should last for about ten minutes.

Warm-up activities should be slow and easy.

Why do them?

When muscles are warm they stretch more easily. When we want our muscles to work hard there is less chance of them being injured if we have done a warm-up.

Some warm-ups to do.

Jogging slowly   and

Stretching

Work with a partner and try to think of a stretching activity for each of the body parts below. Draw pictures of your activities on the back of this sheet, so you can share them with your class.

shoulders	side	legs
neck	back	ankle

Try your activities as part of a warm-up.

Warm-downs help to get our bodies back to a state of rest, after our sport or fitness activity.

Warm-downs should last for about five minutes.

Warm-downs should be slow and easy.

Why do them?

If our muscles cool too quickly they can become stiff and sore. Warm-downs help to prevent this.

Some warm-downs to do.

Jogging   Stretching   Walking

Write true or false next to these statements about warm-downs.

You should only do stretching exercises. ....
You should jog slowly, walk and stretch your muscles. ....
It is good for your body to cool down quickly. ....
Warm-downs help to make your muscles sore. ....
You should work slowly for about five minutes. ....

You don't have to do special activities to keep fit. Simple, everyday activities are just as good.

Draw a picture in each box to match the captions underneath.

Walking the dog.

Helping in the garden.

Flying a kite.

Playing on the beach.

36

GET FIT WITH AEROBIC DANCE   Name.......................

If you like listening to music, why not exercise while you listen. This will help to keep your heart strong and healthy. You will be able to firm up your muscles as well.

Here are some body actions to get you started. Repeat each body action four or eight times then change to a new action.

Think of some actions for yourself.

You could make up some of your own aerobic dance activities with a friend.

37

GET FIT WITH AN EXERCISE CIRCUIT Name.......................

Exercise circuits are a fun way to improve your fitness. They involve many different activities. You can change from one activity to another as often as you like.

Here is a circuit for you to try.

Do this circuit three times.

Make up your own circuit.

Teacher's Notes

Get Fit With An Exercise Circuit

With the circuit shown children could initially do the following repetitions:

Activity 1   5 repetitions
Activity 2   10 leg changes
Activity 3   4 repetitions
Activity 4   5 repetitions
Activity 5   4 for each leg
Activity 6   20 skips

As children continue with the circuit they could gradually increase the number of repetitions for each activity. It should be pointed out that students with a higher fitness level could start with a greater number of repetitions compared with someone who was at a lower level of fitness.

When children try to make up their own circuits it should be stressed that they include activities from each of the fitness areas: cardiovascular endurance, flexibility, muscular endurance and muscular strength. This ensures a balanced fitness approach.

Measure a distance of 500 metres around your school or oval. Every time you jog 500 metres, or half a kilometre, you may colour in one of the spots on the sneaky snake.

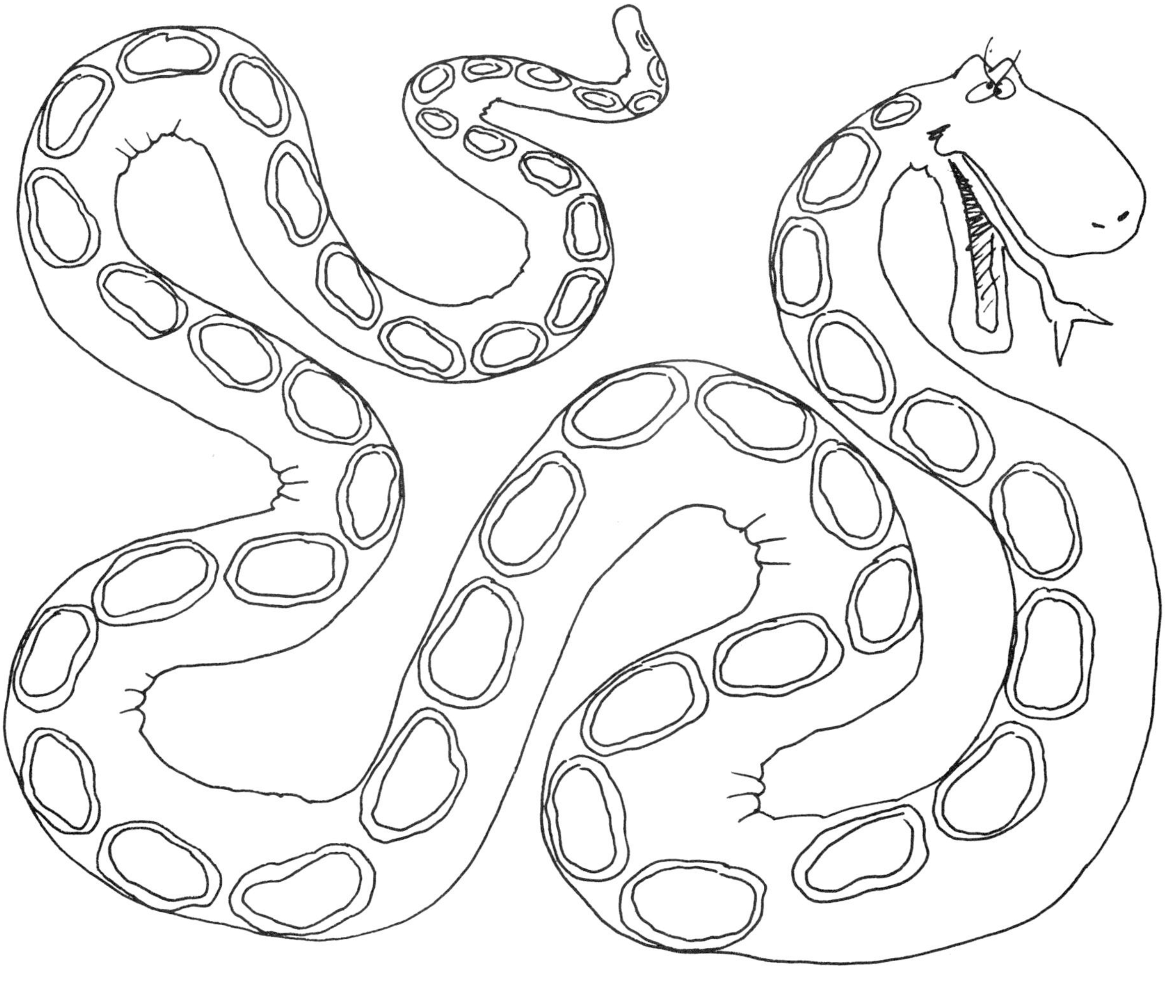

After one month find out how many kilometres have you run. .... km

Many people are not very fit. Why do you think this is so? ....

....

....

....

Some jobs help people to keep fit. For each of the statements below, name the job which would most make a person fit.

(a) secretary or a farmer ....

(b) park ranger or a shopkeeper ....

(c) rubbish collector or a taxi driver ....

(d) dentist or a milkman ....

(e) doctor or a builder ....

Many people work in jobs where they are not very active. These people will need to do extra fitness activities. Discuss some activities that would be helpful for these people. ....

....

....

....

....

....

....

....

THE FITNESS MISTAKE   Name.......................

Read the following carefully to make sure you don't make the big fitness mistake.

The mistake that many people make is that they try to do too much, too soon.

Look at the pictures below. Write down what you think the people might be thinking.

Write down how much of each of the following activities you would do each week if you were starting a fitness programme.

(a) jogging .... km
(b) swimming .... laps
(c) bike riding .... km
(d) skipping .... skips
(e) sit-ups .... (number)

Remember!

Start slowly and easily, then gradually do more.

Exercise must be done correctly if it is to be good for your body.

You can not get fit overnight. It will take time and many exercise sessions. The key to fitness is to start with easy activities and build up slowly.

If you were planning a fitness programme, how much of each of these activities would you do each week? Fill in the boxes below with your answers.

Activity	Week 1	Week 2	Week 3	Week 4	Week 5	Week 6
Jogging (km)						
Skipping (number)						
Sit-ups (number)						
Bike riding (km)						
Swimming (laps)						

KEEPING THE FUN IN FITNESS

Name......................

Many people give up their fitness activity because it stops being fun.

Why do you think this happens to some people? ....
....
....
....
....
....

Name some things you could do to make sure that your fitness work is fun.

....
....
....
....
....
....

Remember!

If it's not fun — change it. Don't give up.

Imagine this is your friend.

What could you do or say to help your friend become more active? Write down some fitness activities which would be good fun to do together. ....

....

....

....

....

....

....

....

....

....

....

HERE TODAY, GONE TOMORROW

Getting fit is hard work. Keeping fit is even harder work. If muscles are not used they shrink and become weak. Muscles which are firm make you look good, they help your posture and assist your performance in sporting activities.

Think!

Name five sports stars who you think would be very fit. ....
....
....

Fitness musts

To keep your muscles firm and to improve the fitness of your heart, you must:

- do fitness activities three to four times each week
- have your heart beating at least 150 times per minute during activities
- exercise for at least thirty minutes each day
- do activities which will use all the muscle groups.

Name one activity that you do, which includes all the fitness musts. ....
....

What to do!

If you strain a muscle or a ligament, hurt a joint or even break a bone, the best **immediate** treatment is **rest** and

I...... This helps to stop the bleeding from injured blood vessels. The more blood that collects in a wound, means an increase in swelling and the longer it takes for the injury to heal. Make sure you don't put the ice directly onto the wound, as it may damage the bare skin.

C...mp......ss......n This helps to stop the bleeding and swelling.

El...v.........on This means getting the injured part of the body above the level of the heart, this helps to drain blood away from the wound.

Teacher's Notes

Injuries

Missing words: **I**ce   **C**ompression   **E**levation

It is important for children to understand, and to be confident in, injury management. Practise can be given in class in the application of ice, compression bandaging, elevation of the injured body part and placing the injured person in a resting position. Children could do this in groups with injury simulations.

FITNESS FUN   Name......................

Can you think of a funny caption to suit each picture?

IS YOUR FITNESS IMPROVING ?

Name.......................

Here is a simple fitness test which you could use every few weeks to check if your fitness is improving.

Test	Measure	Up to 8 years	Up to 10 years
Shuttle run	Time	5 x 10 metres	5 x 15 metres
Run/walk	Time	500 metres	1 000 metres
Standing long jump	Distance		
Bent knee sit-ups	Number in one minute		
Push-ups	Number in one minute	Against a wall	Onto a chair
Sit and reach	Distance		

Be sure that you make your best attempt each time.

Keep your scores on the chart on sheet 48 so you can see how you are improving.

Teacher's Notes

Is Your Fitness Improving?

The fitness tests are recommended measures for the various aspects of fitness. For each of the tests there are some key points to keep in mind when testing students.

Shuttle run

Use witches' hats or markers to set the distance. Children must touch each hat/marker at each end. This ensures that students run the full distance.

Run/walk

The course should be outlined using markers so the students do not take short cuts. The course should be planned so that it does not include many laps as it can become confusing when children try to count and remember completed laps.

Standing long jump

A measuring tape can be taped to the floor. Children line their toes up with the beginning of the tape. The distance jumped can be easily read.

Bent knee sit-ups

It is best that children only lift their head and shoulders from the floor, rather than continue to a sitting up position so as not to risk back injury. The knees must stay in a bent position with feet flat on the floor.

Push-ups

When children do the push-ups their shoulders should be in a position above the hands. The body should be held firm and straight. If the children let their bodies sag too much such attempts should not be counted.

Sit and reach

Children should sit with their legs straight out in front of them and their feet slightly apart. A measuring tape can be taped to the ground. Children place their heels at the beginning of the tape and slowly reach forward pushing a small block of wood with both hands. Distance can then be read from the tape. Some pressure placed on the children's knees may be necessary for a more accurate score.

48

MY FITNESS TEST SCORES   Name........................

Fitness Test	Date	Date	Date	Date
Shuttle run				
Run/walk				
Standing long jump				
Bent knee sit-ups				
Push-ups				
Sit and reach